NO TIME TO CRY

A GLIMPSE AT THE LIFE OF AN EVERY DAY WOMAN

SARAH MUNKACSY

Outskirts Press, Inc.
http://www.outskirtspress.com

Paperback ISBN: 978-1-9772-3229-8
Hardback ISBN: 978-1-9772-3292-2

I dedicate this book in honor of my Aunt Artie and her children. She taught me to love unconditionally, as she loved me beyond measure. She was one of the strongest, most loving, patient, and resilient women I've known. When I have bad years or bad days, she is still my role model. I can't imagine living the life she did and, in the end, the one word I can describe my Aunt Artie with is.....Love.

Foreword

Born on the doorstep of the Great Depression, Ardath Fenn grew up amidst love and struggle. World War II lifted the US out of depression and into a worldwide conflict. She lost her father, a kind and gentle man, while still in high school. From a young age, she was forged into a woman of determination and strength.

She married Dutch Knepp after the war, and they raised five children together. Life was hard, but the couple raised their children, three with special needs, as best they could. Dutch died young, and Ardath's difficult path descended into trials few of us can imagine.

Yet, she laughed and played her music really loud. And in the center of an endless storm, she created a safe space where patience and acceptance lived comfortably with laughter and music. As the portrait of her life unfolds, the colors that shine through are grace, strength, kindness, and love.

Acknowledgments

For my family, friends, and neighbors who have believed in me and encouraged me to tell this story! Frani and Frank, thank you for giving me your place, my "safe haven," as I began. Lottie, thank you for your continued support through the whole spectrum of emotions I experienced during this journey. Al, thanks for allowing me to go on vacation for six years as I wrote this book. Randa, Aunt Joyce, and of course, Mona, Sheila, and Marti, thank you for all of the memories, patience, and trust. Thanks for hanging around through completion! With all my love!

Table of Contents

Foreword i

Acknowledgments iii

Introduction...vii

1. A Strong Foundation 1

2. Oh, How Precious Childhood Would Be 9

3. Adulthood in a Minute 16

4. Hitch with Parenthood.. 24

5. Living Between the Lines of Life and Death 34

6. Beating   the   Odds
   or Striking Out.. 39

7. A Lesson in Living (& Dying)... 43

8. Rock My World in 18 Months.. 46

9. Don't Lie to Me 61

10. Don't Leave Me; I'm Not Ready.. 68

11. Sifting Through the Memories and the Stuff...................... 75

12. Where We Are Today—The Legacy Lives On 81

13. Test of Faith 90

Appendix I.. 92

Introduction

You will find a woman in this book whose life was riddled with more tragedies than any person should endure. You will also find a woman that lived her life without complaints or judgment toward others. Those she knew were accepted and loved just as they were. She greeted every day with a positive outlook and open arms when most of us would cover our heads and wish the world would stop to let us off. You will come to understand just how strong of a woman she was in her faith and in her love for life.

My mother wrote the following letter in December 1965. It is absolutely amazing that the words my mother wrote on my behalf as a child would become one of the greatest truths of my life. I am writing this book to show others what a remarkable woman Ardath Ruth Knepp truly was. The love she expressed to all she encountered and how she led her life evoked inspiration within those who knew her. I intend to carry on the lessons offered through the love and care that Artie modeled. Let me introduce you to my aunt Artie!

To Ardath written by her sister Nona as if being written by 18-month-old Sarah Jane Sprague:

My Dear "Other Mother",

First, I want to wish you a "Merry Christmas"—even if I have been somewhat of a pest while preparing for this special holiday. I had a ball picking at the tree and teasing you—you will never know how much enjoyment I get hearing you bitch at me.

You, dear sweet Mother, have made my first year and a half so wonderful. You have given me such good care and love that I cannot ever repay you for it. My own mother is out in this wide, wild world trying to prove something that I am sure she cannot explain what it is she is after. I feel inside of me that she will never know the affection and love that you and I have for each other.

I know at times I can't be worth the work I have caused you, but you watch me as I grow, and you will find how your love and kindness will show. I require so much love, and you are the person who always has the time to return this love.

I am so sorry that I have bitten Scott or been mean to Randa, but I don't like them when I want your entire attention. I promise I will do better this next year because you will teach me not to be so mean and that your love and kindness cannot stop with just me. (I really love Randa and Scott, but don't you tell them.)

I know life has not been the very best to you, but the good Lord has given us all a reason to be here, and yours is love and to be kindness to others.

Someday, I will tell you just how wonderful you are in your language, but for the time being, or until I want to give up my own language, you must understand, I am telling you I Love You very much.

I love my uncle Dutch also; he has been so kind and good to me. (I would have said "Dutch" before I said "Mommy," but I knew she would pout, and she does that all the time now

when things don't go her way, so to make her feel good, I said
"Mommy" first).

Love,
Your Baby "Sarah"

My Dear "Other Mother";

First I want to wish you a "Merry Christmas" - even if I have been somewhat of a pest while preparing for this special holiday. I had a ball picking at the tree and teasing you - you will never know how much enjoyment I get hearing you bitch at me.

You dear sweet Mother have made my first year and a half so wonderful, you have given me such good care and love that I cannot ever repay you for it. My own Mother is out in this wide, wild world trying to prove something that I am sure she cannot explain what it is she is after. I feel inside of me that she will never know the affection and love that you and I have for each other.

I know at times I cant be worth the work I have caused you but you watch me as I grow and you will find how your love and kindness will show. I require so much love and you are the person who always has the time to return this love.

I am so sorry that I have bitten Scott or been so mean to Branda, but I don't like them when I want your entire attention. I promise I will do better this next year, because you will teach me not to be so mean and that your love and kindness cannot stop with just me (I really love Branda and Scott but don't you tell them)

I know life has not been the very best to you but the good Lord has given us all a reason to be put here and yours is love and kindness to others.

Someday I will tell you just how wonderful you are in your language, but for the time being, or until I want to give up my own language you must understand, I am telling you I love you very much.

I love my Uncle Dutch also, he has been so kind and good to me. (I would have said Dutch before I said Mommy but I knew she would pout and she does that all the time now when things don't go her way, so to make her feel good I said Mommy first).

Love
Your Baby "Sarah"

CHAPTER 1

A Strong Foundation

IT WAS A couple of months after Aunt Artie had passed when Marti and I were in my Suburban headed to Oklahoma to see the girls and go through her remaining belongings. Marti and I were still mourning the loss of our "other" mother. Our luggage was light, taking just the essentials. The last time Marti and I traveled together was the flight we took to say goodbye. That visit was at the forefront of our minds and heavy on our hearts. We couldn't stay in Oklahoma until she passed, so we both felt like we had let her down, and we also felt disappointed in ourselves. We worked full time, had families, and were so busy with our involvement in the schools and our communities that the commitments we held precluded a longer trip.

When we flew down to say goodbye, it was bittersweet. This woman endured so much throughout her lifetime. No one wanted to see her suffer any longer. She was diagnosed with cancer in early December and was given three to six months to live. The family had opted out of treatment, just palliative care and pain management, as she had already been through so much. Nine years earlier, Aunt Artie had a major stroke and lost the use of most of her left side, leaving her confined to a wheelchair. Her life was very restricted, and the quality wasn't excellent. She had a lot of support around the decision to forgo chemotherapy so that we could focus on helping her maintain as much comfort as possible.

When Marti and I arrived, all we had on our minds was to spend as much time with Aunt Artie as possible. She had limited mobility, but her caretaker, Colleen, made sure she was comfortable.

Aunt Artie brought a few of her personal belongings with her to Oklahoma. Among them were three photos, a picture of Scott, one of her and Dutch, and one of her mother. She also had a CD player, a small music box I had given her, and a cherub I made for her many years ago. A lot of light shined through the windows as Marti and I walked into her room. We were both greeted with the twisted smile we had become accustomed to after her stroke. She was overjoyed and almost relieved to see us. We had just arrived as her sister Joyce was leaving to return home to Michigan so that she could have family with her continuously.

Typical of Aunt Artie, she wanted to know how the flight was and how *we* were doing. We filled her in on what seemed trivial at the moment just to please her. I wanted to bawl and hug her while Marti managed to remain stoic. She always leaned toward the lighter side, helping me find humor even in the most difficult situations.

As Marti and I settled into her space, we grabbed chairs and dragged them into the room where we camped out. We took turns in there with her, and we read books, I read the newspaper, and listened to all her favorite music, which mainly consisted of Neil Diamond. I spent some time in the kitchen, making her favorite things to eat. We knew she wouldn't be around for her birthday in February, so I was determined to make her a birthday cake. I had no clue how to make Aunt Artie's favorite angel food cake with maple frosting, so I picked up the phone to call my mom for the recipe.

When I spoke with my mom, I asked her again if she was all right with not seeing Aunt Artie again. She assured me that it was fine. She and Artie talked practically every Saturday morning for hours on end over the telephone, even though they were only blocks away from each other. They could have sat down and had coffee face-to-face, but they always chose to talk on the phone. It always seemed as if they might have been solving the world's problems, and as such, had acquired the label of Ann and Abby (Landers). Mom said that she had told her goodbyes to Artie and preferred not to see her as she was now, so I let it go.

For me, I *had* to be with Aunt Artie during this time. Over the years, Aunt Artie had taught me to stay busy in times of crisis. *"Keep your hands busy so that your heart won't hurt so much as you are doing good in the world."* Busy hands make a happy heart. I made potato salad, the family recipe, which was reminiscent of the years previous. I made cinnamon rolls and the birthday cake she always had. Life is too short not to eat some sweets from time to time. I also made hot beef, a comfort food during hard times. All in all, there was enough food to feed a small army.

The house smelled wonderful, and I was hoping that the smell of her favorite foods would bring back her appetite. When we gave her food, though, she didn't want any, and the majority of the time, she would flat-out refuse to eat. The one thing that she did want to taste was the homemade maple frosting that was on her birthday cake. My heart rejoiced when she told me that it was delicious. I didn't care if she tried anything else. It was miraculous that she wanted to try any-thing at all, and above that, she even liked it! If she had wanted it, I would have given her the whole cake, even if she only ate the frosting off the top.

When I could spend some one-on-one time with my aunt, I wanted to make the best of it. For me, that meant I couldn't cry. She had given me so much and loved me so deeply, I just wanted to love her and make her feel comfortable. I walked into the room, determined not to cry. I wanted to go through some old pictures and reminisce with her, so I grabbed the box lying on the floor and sat down on the bed beside her. Before we walked down memory lane, I asked Artie if there was anything I could get her. She re-sponded by asking for Colleen. I immediately thought the worst and almost panicked, so I hollered for Colleen. At that moment, I didn't feel that she was coming quick enough, so I headed to the kitchen to get her.

Colleen and I almost ran into each other, coming around the corner. She sauntered her way around Aunt Artie's bed. It should be noted that Colleen isn't by any means a small woman. My father would have called her an Amazon woman or a gentle giant. She stands about six foot tow, weighs around 200 pounds give or take, and likely wears size 12 shoes. When she got to the end of the bed, she said, "What do ya need, Artie?" with her Oklahoma accent.

Aunt Artie responded, "A hug."

I didn't know how to react or respond, so the first words out of my mouth were, "What am I, chopped liver?" I was sitting right there. I would have loved to hug her! Then I looked at Colleen as she wrapped her arms around my aunt and gently lifted her upper torso off the bed ever so carefully and hugged her firmly, to which I then said, out loud, "You bitch!" In that truly loving moment, I was assured that my aunt, my "other mother," was in the best hands.

Randa was in the doorway, Marti standing behind her, and we all just busted out laughing. That helped me let down my guard around Colleen and begin to allow myself to see the bond they had built in a relatively short time, a bond that I wanted to understand and would take time to do so out of love and respect for Aunt Artie.

Colleen

I was able to spend many hours with Aunt Artie. I rubbed cream on her dry arms and legs and gave her sips of water. I massaged her shoulders as I had done so many times since I was a little girl. We listened to music, looked at pictures, read, and sometimes, I just sat there watching her as she drifted in and out of sleep. Most of the sleeping was due to the pain patch that was on her shoulder. Colleen had taught us how to rub it to release the medicine when we saw her wincing or looking uncomfortable.

I was so selfish, but I wanted to keep her alert and talking and sharing for as long as I possibly could. I didn't want her slipping away from me. There was a time when I knew that she was peaceful, and I wasn't sure if she was sleeping or not, but I shared a memory with her at that moment. I told her that I remembered being at the hospital with her after her stroke and telling her that I wasn't ready to lose her. I know that she was tired and had been through so much, but I didn't want her to leave me. I told her then that if she was ready, I understood, but I didn't want to lose her. This time, there was no selfishness! This was about her, *not* me. More than anything, I didn't want her to be in pain anymore. I assured her that I would do my best to help take care of Randa and keep the family together, nurturing them as she had nurtured us.

I slept right outside her bedroom on a small love seat. I didn't sleep much. I was listening to her breathing, and the cat was driving me crazy, playing with the drapes. What little sleep I did get was more like just resting my eyes. I was pretty close to her bedroom, so I was very aware of her sounds. At one point, I heard something that I didn't like, so I got up to check on her. I had never really experienced this kind of stuff before, seeing a really sick person, so I didn't know what to expect. I wanted to know so many things and had spent some time asking Colleen questions as we sat at the kitchen table. When I went into her room, she was foaming at the mouth. Needless to say, that scared the daylights out of me, so I headed to Colleen at 2:30 in the morning.

Colleen came in to take her vitals and just looked at me and said it was "part of the process." Given it was in the middle of the night, Colleen didn't want to talk with me, so I just lay awake for most of the night, thinking and remembering all of the times with my aunt. How could I fit it all in? How could I avoid wasting another moment? How could I tell her everything that was still left unsaid?

Morning finally came, but it seemed like it took forever. I needed to tell her. I needed her to know just how much of an impact she had on my life! I knew she hadn't rested well at all, so when daylight broke, I went in ever so quietly. When I knew she was a little more awake and alert, I started my memories off with when we took care of our family graves. Of all places to start, right? Well, it made sense to me. When we took care of their graves, we paid our respects and celebrated their lives. We always took wine with us to drink as we planted flowers. Sometimes, we would lie down on the grass and make pictures out of the clouds in the sky. The two of us had shared so many memorable moments throughout my life, and I'd learned so many of life's lessons just by experiencing them, not talking about them. This had been another one of those moments.

One of the things that describe her most without it sounding too pitiful would be long-suffering. The physical pain she endured was tremendous, but the emotional pain was also unimaginable. She never asked, "Why me, Lord?" She never complained about the pain, the agony, the disappointments, the lack of sleep, the lack of absolutely any private time, including when she went to bed. How do I tell her that the love and compassion that I have for people and the critters of the world came from her? How do I tell her that the patience that I have for some of the silliest, stupidest things came from watching her? How do I tell her that looking at life as the "glass half full" came from her? I realized through these few days together that I didn't need to tell her. She already knew. She knew me better than anyone. She was the first person in my life that knew me better than I knew myself. She was the one who taught me unconditional love. Love doesn't end with death. It's just another way of living your virtues. Patience, until we meet again.

A picnic is a state of mind & can be made anywhere.

Cookie Jar

CHAPTER 2

Oh, How Precious Childhood Would Be . . .

ARDATH RUTH FENN was born on March 25, 1924, to Eunice and Kenneth (Ki) Fenn, at 218 West Lincoln, Ionia, Michigan, at 4:00 in the morning. This sweet little one weighed in at five pounds, five ounces, and 20 inches long. No parents could be happier than Ki and Eunice. The new parents loved their baby girl, and it showed through their nurturing and attentiveness. Ardath had her "firsts" just as every child does; however, she seemed to have an innate determination to learn and explore. She sat up at six and a half months, climbed up to chairs, and played patty-cake at eight months. She also learned to crawl at nine months and was standing alone at 12 months. Ardath used a potty chair and started walking at 14 months. She had her first tooth at 15 months and quit using the bottle at 20 months old. It is comical to know that her first word at 10 months old was "Kitty-Kitty." It was comical only because Ardath absolutely loved animals, as everyone came to understand as she got older.

For her first Christmas, she received all kinds of gifts . . . five dresses, a pair of wool stockings, a piggy bank, jingle bells, a stuffed rabbit and kitty, and a new baby plate. There was no shortage of holiday cheer in the Fenn family. Ardath's first birthday was celebrated at Aunt Ruth and Uncle Case's house, Eunice's brother and sister-in-law.

For many people, Ardath's firsts were important to others who were watching her grow. Unbeknownst to all, Ardath's first experiences would become more important in time, especially to be documented by Eunice in 1924, a record that would be referred to so many times in her life and ours.

Baby Ardath's 1st picture

Ardath's sister, Joyce Margaret, joined the family on November 7, 1925. This was the beginning of a beautiful sisterhood and friendship that would last a lifetime. These two sisters had a head start on the others, and that, in part, was what bonded them. They had six years alone together before the next sibling came along. Audrey Rachel joined them on January 26, 1931. A little over a year later, Winona Gail was born on May 25, 1932. The baby of the family, Sandra Jean, was born on October 27, 1938. They were five beautiful girls who were devoted daughters and sisters through life's journeys.

Younger Fenn Girls

When Ardath and Joyce were nine and eight, the family lived at the house by the dam in Mio, Michigan. One of the family rules was that the girls were not supposed to cross the road because of the danger posed by the creek. Ardath, with her adventurous and curious side, wanted to cross the street one day and explore the unknown. She talked Joyce into going with her. However, when they returned, their dad was standing on the bottom step of the porch. He had the girls' jump rope in his hands, and they could see it as they headed slowly back toward the house. Anticipating they were going to get their butts whipped, they were quite shaken. When they got closer to the porch, he chewed them out and made sure they knew never to cross the road again. Then he told them to go jump rope. Ki was kind with an easygoing demeanor. No one remembers seeing him angry, and he was very lenient with the girls. Eunice, known by the family in later years as "The General," was the disciplinarian.

Ki worked for Consumers Power, where he repaired dams all over Michigan. His assignment at the time was in Mio, Michigan. He smoked a pipe and drank whiskey and always had a pint in the cupboard. When he had to cut wood on Saturdays, he would take a nip out of the bottle. Ki was a frequent customer of Grover's saloon during the week after work and on the weekends. Eunice often told the story that on one particular Saturday, he didn't come home, so she went uptown looking for him, and as she walked in, he was singing, "Who's Afraid of the Big Bad Wolf." At the thought of his performance, everybody laughed.

Eunice and Ki also boarded people that worked on the Mio dam for Consumers Power. They did this to help pay the bills and help others with a place to stay. Eunice was a grammar school teacher at the time, so the supplemental income helped them make ends meet. On Saturday, the girls helped their mom get Sunday dinner ready. The girls caught one of their chickens, then Eunice would take it over to the stump and cut off the chicken's head with an ax. Next, she would hang the chicken on the clothesline to let the blood drain. Then they would singe the skin of the chicken and put it in boiling water.

The Sunday dinners fed 10–12 family members and tenants. Eunice would prepare the dinner, always creating a mess with frying grease from the chicken, the preparation of the gravy, the endless side dishes, and the pies. After dinner, the adults would get up and go in the sitting room to visit while Nona and Audrey were left to clean up the mess.

In those times, everyone had a job, even if it was helping around the house. The girls earned money by picking potato bugs off the plants. Artie hated working outside. She preferred to stay inside to dust or clean the floors, while Joyce went outside to help her father with other tasks.

Right before the Fenns moved to Mio, Ardath had just finished fourth grade, and Joyce finished third grade. When they arrived in the new town, the school let Joyce "skip" fourth grade and move up with her sister. In the fall, the girls started fifth grade together.

Every summer, the family traveled to Matherton, where Eunice's sister, Letha, lived. Letha's husband, John Gage, lent Ki and Eunice his horse so they could use it to cultivate their garden for the entire summer. The girls worked hard as soon it was daylight, hauling hay and tending to the garden.

Part of the girls' responsibilities was mowing the yard with hand mowers during the warm months. They always seemed to find a way to make their chores fun. The girls usually had at least one sister to do the chores with. Washing the laundry and hanging the clothes on the line was a two-person job and something they could do while playing hide-and-seek. Doing the dishes meant one would wash while the other dried. Sweeping the floors and shaking the rugs became a game to see who could snap the rugs the loudest.

While the girls shared a strong resemblance, their personalities varied greatly. Nona was quite the dancer. As a young child, she liked to watch herself perform, so she danced on the back of the toilet where there was a mirror. One day while doing her daily dance session, she broke the toilet tank top. These were among the instances where the girls were fortunate to have such a mild-tempered father.

From the time Nona was a child, all the way through her life, she was full of energy. She could hardly sit still. Nona loved to play and tease the other kids. Aside from her playful side, that bundle of energy was always eager to help her parents in any way she could. Being a people pleaser, she worked hard around the house and spent time working outdoors with her father. She always managed to find ways to make the work as fun as possible.

Audrey had little modesty. One morning when she got up, she strolled into the bathroom butt naked and walked in on one of the boarders, not thinking anything of it, and said, "I gotta go potty." She suffered from convulsions, especially when she spiked a fever. The convulsions continued into adulthood. Later, she was diagnosed with epilepsy. There were times that the seizures were traumatic for the entire family.

At times, Joyce would run away because she couldn't be around when Audrey was having seizures. Audrey was also well known for having a short fuse. She would fly off the handle at the littlest of things, and her temper was horrific. Sometimes, she would hit her sisters or throw anything nearby. The other girls often described her as outright mean.

Sandy was mellow, outgoing, and a sweetheart. **She was born with a smile, and that remained her demeanor throughout childhood.**

Artie was the troublemaker. She liked to have fun. Artie always had more fun with the boys than the girls. The boys dared her to go hand over hand under the bridge in Mio, and she could do it with the best of them. She would not be outdone.

When the kids were younger, they hardly ever went to church, but the family would often go for the holidays. Aunt Ruth and Uncle Case came to get the girls and bought them dresses at Jacobson's. At Christmas, the girls made candy and sewed clothing.

Several ladies owned the grocery store in Mio, who allowed Ki and Eunice to have a bill they ran from week to week. Ki settled up each payday.

Ardath was fun-loving and petite. But one day, she was late for class because the boys picked her up, stuffed her into a garbage can, and she couldn't get out.

Ki and Eunice went to Grandma Goodwin's and asked the two Wright sisters to stay with the girls. Eunice and Ki left some money on the buffet for the children. Joyce wanted to get some candy, but Artie had already taken the money to buy cigarettes. Joyce was not happy, not happy at all, not only because her sister and friend didn't bring her back any candy, but she was smoking cigarettes now.

The two eldest daughters would go out together and come home late. Sometimes, Artie would wake up her parents with her giggling. One morning after such an incident, Eunice told the girls to stop the giggling when they came home, or they were going to get into trouble. Ardath was a junior in high school when she went uptown on a Sunday afternoon to meet up with her classmate, Bessie, and some boys. The boys asked if the girls wanted to go for a ride. The girls got in the car and made the four-hour, round-trip drive to Flint from Mio. They were gone all day and half of the night! Artie was supposed to babysit that evening, and when she didn't show up, Joyce had to fill in for her. Ki and Eunice were extremely worried.

Joyce got home about midnight, still miffed at having to take Artie's babysitting job. When she walked in and found that Artie still wasn't home, her anger turned into fear. Eunice had gone to check on the rest of the girls when Artie strolled in around 2:30 a.m. Artie couldn't understand why everyone was so upset. Needless to say, she was grounded for quite some time.

During the time Artie was grounded, there was a special dance at the high school. They had gotten new dresses for the occasion, but Ki told Ardath that she wasn't going. Joyce was feeling sorry for both Artie and herself. If Ardath couldn't attend, it certainly wouldn't have been as much fun. About 20 minutes before the dance, Ki went to get the dress and told Artie, "Oh, go put this on and go to the dance."

Ardath was the oldest. She was able to see all of the things that happened with each of the girls. Ardath had always said that she didn't want to get married, and she didn't want to have any kids, likely because she knew that she had caused so much concern and worry for her parents. **She just wanted to have fun, and she thought that marriage and kids took all the fun away.**

CHAPTER 3

Adulthood in a Minute

KI AND EUNICE both had rheumatic fever when they were youngsters. No one knew it could cause problems in the future, so they lived their lives like anyone else. The year that Ki turned 38, he started having some difficulty breathing, so Eunice insisted that he seek medical attention. The doctor explained to him that extensive damage had occurred to his heart. Ki was also told that he was not to climb the steps at the dam where he worked. The doctor also advised Ki and Eunice against taking on any more debt. "There's no hope for recovery," he told them.

"Recovery of what?" asked Eunice, and the doctor replied, "Heart failure." The damage to Ki's heart was irreparable. At that time, they diagnosed him with a "sick" heart.

Ki and Eunice returned home very somber. Ki promised to talk to Consumer's Power about his job. The two also discussed telling the girls and Kenneth's family. Ki made Eunice promise that she wouldn't tell the Fenn side of the family.

As far as telling the girls, what could they say? How do you tell them that Daddy might not be around to see the oldest two graduate next year? How do you tell your two-year-old that Daddy won't be able to play with you much longer? How do you tell the middle two that they need to get along and that all of them were going to have to help their mother?

The hours and days that passed were hard. Ki wanted to be present for every single moment with his girls, but he knew that he still needed to work and bring home money to live. When he spoke to his employer, they offered him a desk job in Saginaw. Ki went home and talked with Eunice about his concern for moving the girls to a city. He didn't think it was fair to uproot the girls for a desk job, so they stayed in Mio, and he continued to do the best he could.

Ki needed to get his affairs in order. They had just purchased a new car for $800, so as for new debt, that was water under the bridge. He needed to make sure Eunice and the girls were taken care of. One of Ki's brothers, Freddy, 21 at the time, was one of their boarders. Ki called Freddy to speak with him privately about taking care of Eunice and the girls once he was gone. Freddy solemnly swore to do what's best for the family after his brother had passed.

In the fall, Ki became quite ill and was seeing Dr. Jardine in West Branch. The doctor told him there was nothing they could do for him, so they sent him home to bed to die. In January, he was down with a bad cold. The family planned to take him to the hospital in Ann Arbor. The man at the county commission, Bobeer, was the one who would bring Ki to Ann Arbor. He was supposed to come at noon. In the morning before school, Ki called all the kids into the bedroom before leaving. Eunice asked Joyce to stay home from school that day as she would accompany Ki to Ann Arbor, and someone needed to be home to take care of the daily chores. Eunice sent Freddy upstairs to check on Ki around 11:30 a.m. and found him dead in their bed.

The hours and days that came after were a blur to the whole family. At 37, Eunice was a widow with five beautiful girls to raise on her own. Her first task would be the hardest. This newly single mother had to break the devastating news to her children. Then she had to arrange to bury her husband.

Ardath, 17, and Joyce, 16, were home when their dad died, so they could spend time with their mother alone before the other girls got home. The three of them made a pact to stick together and see each other through the hard times to come.

The girls watched as their mother fell apart on her brother, Case's, shoulder. She sobbed uncontrollably, asking Case how she was going to do it. How was she going to get through this? How was she going to raise five girls, have a job, and take care of the house on her own? How was she going to survive this?

These unanswered questions loomed over Eunice like a rainy day that never seemed to end.

"... little minds tend to draw conclusions that will help them get through a crisis."

When the younger girls got home from school, Eunice sat down with them to say some of the most painful words she ever imagined having to tell them. Through her tears, nine-year-old Nona asked her mother if she would ever see her father again. Eunice assured Nona, "Yes, of course, honey, you will see your father again." It was many years later when Nona was able to express her expectation of seeing her father on the street or places they visited. At the time, she didn't know that it would be in heaven where she would see him again. Without in-depth explanations, little minds tend to draw conclusions that will help them get through a crisis. In Nona's naivete, she was able to hold on to hope to get through the loss she hadn't fully understood yet.

Ki was a tall man, and the casket they chose for him was at the community hall in nearby Matherton. People came to pay their respects. The ladies that owned the small grocery store brought boxes and boxes of food to help this struggling family that had been faithful patrons of their business. The Fenn side of the family was bitter toward Eunice because neither she nor Ki told them just how serious Ki's heart problems were. The extended family felt robbed of the knowledge that their loved one was given a terminal prognosis. The decision to not share Ki's illness with his family proved to be one mistake that would haunt them for a very long time. The repercussions that Eunice faced from the Fenn family lasted generations.

During the service, Joyce and Audrey sat side by side. Audrey started to cry, then Joyce did as well. Artie and Joyce still had one more year of high school to get through. Freddy was living with the Fenns. He was only 21 when his brother died. Ki's little brother, barely old enough to be called a man, was asked to take on this enormous responsibility. While he was well intended to serve his late brother as he had promised, it was too much for him to be responsible for.

About three weeks after Ki died, Eunice and the family moved into a farmhouse just north of Mio. As spring arrived, they moved back to Mio to live in the upstairs of an old bank building and stayed there until Joyce and Ardath graduated high school.

It wasn't too long after the death of Ki that Freddy started to drink heavily and stopped helping with the chores around the house or even providing any amount of financial support. Eunice was put into the uncomfortable position of confronting her brother-in-law on the matter and asking him to leave. It was another heartache that needed to be endured so she could move on with her life.

Eunice took on a job as a cook in The Log Cabin restaurant in Mio. She had received a widow's pension of $15 a month for each of the girls, which was a needed source of income but wasn't enough to make ends meet. Eunice and Joyce worked at the restaurant together. Ted and Daisy Wright, locals and family friends, owned the restaurant. They paid them each $10 weekly. While Eunice and Joyce worked, Artie stayed at home with the other girls to babysit.

The girls who were old enough to understand the scope of the situation felt sorry for their mother because she worked tirelessly to support the family and didn't have time for much else. Eunice cried every time she was alone, trying to uphold a strong front around her children. **Despite her efforts, the girls heard her at night as she sobbed in her empty bed.**

Joyce often chose not to go out with her friends to make herself more available for her struggling family. She didn't attend her senior prom because she didn't want to leave her mother alone. Joyce recognized that the times when Eunice was alone were the hardest of them all. The family lived close to town and would go home straight after work to sleep, only to continue with the same schedule the next day. It was a frequent occurrence of being awakened by the drunks after the bars closed at night. After weeks of disrupted sleep, Eunice had the idea to make light of the situation. She suggested that anyone who was still awake could sit by the window to watch and listen to the drunks. This provided entertainment for the family and helped distract from their hardships, if only for a little bit.

Things continued to grow harder and harder. Eventually, they were no longer able to stay at the house because of their inability to financially and physically take care of themselves. They had no support from the family around them and decided that being downstate would be more helpful all the way around, not just for Eunice but for the entire family.

The grieving mother and her five girls packed up and moved into a one-bedroom cabin because money was tight. They had someone with a big truck come to move all the big furniture, so they didn't have to do the heavy lifting.

That summer, they went up to Utica to get the rest of their belongings and brought them down to the cabin. That year, Eunice got a job at the mental institution. Sandy was only three when the family moved downstate. That winter, Eunice went to work at the state hospital in the laundry department. For a woman to hold that type of position with such great pay was nothing short of impressive. Audrey and Nona had to shovel the snow and push her car out of the driveway each morning so she could get to work by 5:00 a.m. Eunice worked this job from 1942 to 1946, through all of World War II to VJ Day. She thoroughly enjoyed her work, and she stayed there until she retired due to heart problems. She was put on disability and received a pension from the state hospital. Later, she and her adult children went trailer shopping, and Eunice bought a mobile home in 1961.

Joyce and Ardath went to Grand Rapids to business school and then went to Ann Arbor, where they got jobs. The two would go home on the weekends to visit Eunice and the other girls. While they were away at school, Eunice gave them five dollars a week for expenses. When they would visit home, the girls took canned fruit, bread, and butter back to school with them. The money was supposed to be spent on groceries. Instead, they had popcorn night after night or went to get a Coke, which meant they had enough money to go to the movies.

Cooking wasn't allowed in their rooms, but they did a little. Artie and Joyce moved into their own apartment where they could cook and were there for a while until Artie went back home because she was homesick. Joyce kept her job in Ann Arbor and worked from 8 a.m. to 6:00 p.m., earning $16 a week for wages. Artie had a job at AC Spark Plug in Ionia, and she worked for the war effort.

Joyce had started dating Russell McGregor while she was a senior in high school, and Ardath started dating William (Dutch) Knepp after graduation.

Dutch and Ardath

McGregor/Knepps

When Russell proposed to Joyce, they knew they needed to get permission from Eunice, so they drove down for a visit. Eunice wasn't pleased at all. Uncle Case came to talk with Eunice and explained that she really needed to give her blessings as the kids would get married with or without her acceptance. On May 8, 1943, Joyce and Russ were married at the Smith farm, the ol' homestead.

Ardath and William (Dutch) were also married on the Smith farm on February 25, 1944. Aunt Ruth and Uncle Case tood up with them. Nona, Audrey, Sandra and Grandma Goodwin were there. It was a cold day in Michigan but luckily no snow for the celebration.

Dutch and Ardath

CHAPTER 4

Hitch with Parenthood

ARDATH HAD TO quit work when she found out she was pregnant. At the time, women weren't allowed to be pregnant and work. Dutch and Ardath had a normal birth and brought home Kenneth Lloyd Knepp on April 9, 1945. He was a precious little baby and the first grandchild born on the Fenn side of the family.

Kenny

Kenny began to grow but developed in a few ways that seemed peculiar to these new parents. The little one rocked back and forth on his hands and knees, and when he began to crawl, he crawled backward. They really began to wonder if something was wrong when they changed his diaper, and he did not attempt to try to put his legs down. They took him to their family doctor in Rose City. The doctor was inclined to think that this might be something serious. The doctor suggested that they take Kenny to Ann Arbor, where they could find more specialized doctors.

Artie was pregnant with their second child at the time and took Kenny to Ann Arbor, where they ran a battery of tests and discovered that Kenny had something known as muscular dystrophy (MD). Kenny was about 16 months old when he was officially diagnosed. **Scared out of her mind, Artie was soon to be expecting another baby and wondering if this one would have it too.** When Artie spoke to the doctors, they said that it was such a small chance that any other baby would be afflicted with this disease, which brought some comfort at that time.

Dutch was in the hospital after having his appendix removed when Artie went into labor, so Joyce took Ardath to the hospital to deliver the baby. Sheila Joy Knepp was born on March 30, 1947.

"... there was only time to live in the moment."

Artie and Kenny

Not much was known about muscular dystrophy at the time, but the physical tasks started to bear down on Ardath. MD robs people of the ability to do the simplest tasks. Simple things like brushing their teeth, combing their hair, dressing, and going to the bathroom on their own were things that someone with MD could not do alone. When you watch most kids grow, these are day-to-day tasks that parents celebrate. With Kenny, there weren't a lot of firsts. He wouldn't crawl, he wouldn't stand up, and there were many more firsts he would never get to experience.

Ardath had a two-year-old that had some of the same physical needs as her newborn baby. All that was known for sure was that Kenny's muscles would get weaker and weaker with time. There wasn't time to ponder the "what-ifs" and "what will be." **There was only time to live in the moment.**

Dutch would run around town doing errands and put Kenny in the back window of the car so that he could look around. They would often do this together.

Dutch, Kenny & Roger

At that time, Ardath and Dutch didn't have the money for a wheelchair, so they propped Kenny up with a couple of pillows and towed him around in a red wagon. The wagon became Kenny's mobility to see a little more of the world. What he couldn't have and didn't have in the form of his physical abilities, he certainly made up for with his voice, his interests, his imagination, and his personality. He would never know what it was like to walk or run, go on a date, or hit a baseball. He was going to get everyone else to do things for him and with him!

They lived in a very small cinder block house without indoor plumbing. Artie had a pump that allowed her to pump water into the home, and then she would heat it to bathe the kids. Someone gifted Kenny with a toy fishing pole but put a real hook in it, and as he was playing with it one day, his lip got caught on the fishhook. Ardath picked Kenny up and ran to their neighbors for help to get the hook out of Kenny's lip . . . and completely forgot about Sheila. She was shut inside the house and couldn't open the door or even see out the windows. The little one cried and cried and was so scared because she didn't know where her mom or Kenny had gone in such a hurry, leaving her behind. To Sheila, it seemed like an eternity until the daughter of the neighbor came to get her and take her to her mother.

A neighbor lady bought the family their first TV just for Kenny. TV became a really big thing for him. It allowed him to develop more of an imagination and live vicariously through the TV. Kenny couldn't wait to see his shows on Saturday mornings. *My Friend Flicka, Sky King, Roy Rogers,* and *The Gene Autry Show* were his favorites. Sheila was not allowed to disturb Kenny while his shows were on. He would either be propped up in a chair or on a table watching TV. This pastime became one of the most significant parts of his life. He also got lots of ideas for things the neighbor kids could do when they all got together.

Nona took Kenny to the fair in the wagon, and people made comments about that "mean person not letting that kid sit up," and Kenny thought it was funny. **People with disabilities were looked at strangely, but Kenny either laughed at them . . . or cursed at them. It just depended on his disposition at the time.**

Their cousin Roger McGregor was born in October of the same year as Kenny, so the two were the best of buds, being only months apart in age. Kenny's imagination got a whole bunch of them in trouble many times. He loved to play cops and robbers! His best nemesis was his cousin, Roger James.

Kenny was always adventurous and rather bossy. One might even go as far as to say manipulative. His imagination took him anywhere, and as long as he had willing participants to help, he was all set. As any big brother would, he always told Sheila what to do, and, of course, she always did what Kenny told her to do. Roger's cousins, "the McGregor boys," as they were always called, hung out at the Knepps.

One night when Artie went out with Joyce and Audrey, the kids were standing on the stairway landing and pretending that they were swinging over a river in the jungle. They accomplished this by hanging onto the chandelier and swinging across, then returning to the landing of the stairway. All the McGregor boys did it first, and then it was Sheila's turn. She made it back to the landing, and right after her feet were firmly planted on the landing, the chandelier came crashing to the floor. Of course, this was all prompted by Kenny's imagination. It would be no surprise to find out that Sheila got in trouble despite it being her brother's idea! Dutch confessed that it was so hard for him not to laugh when he figured out what had transpired.

Dutch was teaching the boys how to hit a baseball by throwing the ball up in the air and striking it with the bat. Next thing you know, the ball was flying through one of the windows of the courthouse. Artie was so afraid Dutch would get fired for breaking the window that she came out of the house, scolding all of them, especially Dutch.

Everyone wanted to make Kenny happy, so they always did whatever he wanted.

Sheila and Kenny

Roger, Sheila, and Kenny headed across the field one day with Kenny in a wagon, and he wanted to go really fast. The quicker Sheila and Roger went, the wobblier the wagon became, and they soon dumped Kenny into a sand pile. The two kids couldn't lift him back into the wagon, so they had to run back and get Artie to help them. When they lifted Kenny, his entire front was covered in sand, and all he could do was laugh.

A game of cowboys and Indians . . . what a better place to play than the jail! The four McGregor boys—Joe, Butch, Tim, and Bob—would go to the jail and play cowboys and Indians, locking themselves into the cells. The kids would run upstairs, shooting at each other down the banister.

The boys' idea of fun included terrorizing Sheila. Roger, carrying Kenny, would get a butter knife and chase her. Roger would often hide in the closet, jumping out to scare Sheila. Kenny didn't pay any attention when Artie would get mad. It never seemed to help. Kenny would have Roger be his "hit man." Anything that Kenny wanted to be done, he would put Roger up to it. Over time, Kenny developed physical deformities because of the way his body lay. He wouldn't have been able to sit up in a wheelchair even if they had one at this point in his life. Kenny was limited in what he was able to do compared to his peers due to muscular dystrophy. After the age of five, he couldn't sit up much at all anymore, and without a wheelchair, it was pretty hard to maneuver him.

There was a hill by the jail, and Roger pulled Kenny up it, then Roger would jump in the wagon, and the two of them would fly down the hill! The faster they went, the more fun it was. If they wiped out, Roger would pick Kenny up and throw him back in the wagon. The more adventurous, scary, or dangerous, the better it was for Kenny. With no control over his body or muscles, he quickly learned how to have everyone help him live his life to the fullest. Kenny loved to swear, and, man, *did* he swear. He didn't care who heard him or what their reaction was. He often would tell Roger, "If I could walk, I'd kick your ass."

Roger started smoking at a really young age, and he was afraid Kenny would tell on him, so Roger got Kenny hooked on smoking as well.

Kenny was a baseball freak; he knew baseball inside and out. His favorite team was the Tigers. He even knew their batting averages off the top of his head. Aunt Audrey took Kenny to all the basketball games as well when they were up north.

The sisters would get together and play poker, and they even taught Kenny to play. He had the stamina to outplay anybody. He would swear up a storm as they played poker on the weekend get-togethers.

Kenny was probably only four feet long and had a small frame. He had a thin waist, and his arms and legs weren't more than skin and bones. He didn't have any muscle definition throughout his chest cavity, and he had long, skinny fingers.

The family grew larger when Ramona (Mona) Lynn was born on March 10, 1951. While Artie and Dutch had their hands full with

Kenny's MD continuing to worsen, a series of crises, large and small, occurred.

Mona and Sheila packed lunches and went down to the creek on Aunt Ruth and Uncle Case's property. One of their regular outings while living in northern Michigan was to go to Smith Lake on the weekends. Artie was carrying Kenny while Sheila was walking with Mona, who was three. Mona ran ahead directly into the water and almost drowned. She had bobbed up and down three times before Ardath lay Kenny down in the grass and ran into the water to save her.

When Sheila was five, she got rheumatic fever and was in bed for months before she recuperated. Mona tried to play with her, but Sheila had to stay in bed and rest, no easy feat for a young child even if she wasn't feeling well. At age six, Sheila had a pot of boiling water accidentally dumped on her foot when someone bumped the handle of the pan still on the stove. Sheila's foot got a nasty blister on it from the burn, leaving her on crutches for a while as her foot healed.

Mona would let herself outside if the door weren't latched, and one day, she ran to the drugstore. Mona had taken her diaper off, and Artie found it outside. In a panic, Ardath hollered out to see if any of the neighbors had seen Mona. Luckily, someone called from the local drugstore, saying Mona was there. She had gone to the back of the drugstore to get some ice cream. Ardath found her sitting on a fountain stool, eating her treat.

Randa Rae was born on April 5, 1955. Throughout the pregnancy, Ardath was still concerned about muscular dystrophy, even though the doctors assured her there were low chances of it occurring with the other children. The doctors also told her that it rarely ever affected females, so after having Sheila and Mona, Artie thought that this new baby girl was just fine, and her fears were squelched. However, within the first six months of her life, some of the same physical markers Kenny had resembled Randa's. How could this be happening again?

Randa was able to get into a wheelchair by the time she was three, and that made mobility a little easier for her. Having mobility and sitting upright are two very important things for people with muscular dystrophy so that their muscles don't break down as quickly, and their lungs stay stronger, preventing fluid from settling in them.

At this point, Artie had four kids under the age of 12, two with infantile needs. Kenny and Randa needed to be put on a bedpan, wiped, fed, assisted in brushing their teeth, brushing their hair, and getting dressed. Most day-to-day tasks required assistance. Even sleeping was challenging because they would have to be rolled over in the middle of the night when they would get stiff or cramped.

Three years later, Artie found out she was pregnant with Scott. Nona took her to St. John's to see if they could find a doctor who would give her an abortion, but it was illegal at the time. On March 27, 1958, Scott Russell was born. He too had muscular dystrophy.

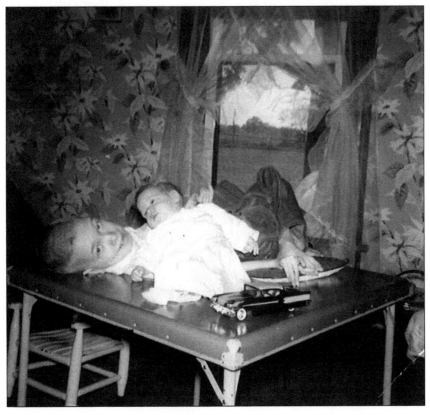

Kenny and Scott

CHAPTER 5

Living Between the Lines of Life and Death

Kenny, The Oldest, Never to Be Forgotten

KENNY WAS NEVER able to go to school because of how compromised his immune system was. Because of this symptom of muscular dystrophy, he was highly susceptible to catching every cold or flu that came into town. With each sickness, his muscles deteriorated more and more. At the time, it wasn't known that it was worse to have a person with muscular dystrophy often lie down. This was a problem because it resulted in quicker deterioration of the muscles and a buildup of fluid in the lungs.

Kenny stopped sitting up at the age of five, and each cold, bout of pneumonia, tonsillitis, and flu seemed to intensify with time. It got to the point where he was sick most of the year. With Sheila and Mona in school, they would come home with lots of cooties from their classmates and spread them through the family.

Kenny had a table that he lay on with a pad on it, and that's where he spent most of his time over the last year of his life. Sometimes, he lay in a chair with his head on the arm of the chair, and his legs draped over the other arm. He could still lie in the red wagon and get pulled around, which was always a highlight for him.

Artie would get up every day and put Kenny on the bedpan, get him dressed, and move him from the bedroom into the living room.

She didn't find much time to stop and enjoy the little things in life, like enjoying flowers on a spring day or getting coffee with friends. Despite the never-ending motherly duties, she truly loved being with her kids. As things got worse for Kenny and closer to the end, all Artie wanted was for her son to live. If Kenny didn't live, how could she hold on to the hope and faith that the other two were going to be okay?

Kenny on porch

Mona and Sheila

Kenny and Sheila

On March 9, 1960, Kenny died. He was just one month shy of his fifteenth birthday. Aunt Artie tried to give Kenny mouth-to-mouth resuscitation to revive him. He had been in the hospital with pneumonia and was released that morning. Then he aspirated and actually swallowed his tongue. Aunt Artie wasn't able to revive him.

Boisterous, full of vim and vigor, he never let muscular dystrophy bother him. He loved to play cards, he was always on the go, and ready for just about anything . . . anything except dying.

Sheila Joy—The Caretaker

Childhood

Sheila was always taking care of everyone else even though she craved and needed love, affection, and acceptance. Sheila always wore her heart on her sleeve and was hurt very easily. She was always looking for attention as a child but never received much. Sheila was always helping her mother with the other kids.

> *". . . we all needed to learn to give and help more than we would receive."*

Early Womanhood

Her passions ran deep; she needed to be loved unconditionally. No man in her life ever fulfilled these needs. The closest she got to get what she needed was her father as she became an adult. However, that chapter was short-lived. Sheila got pregnant at age 17 by a fellow named Mike, but they never married. This was such a hard time for Sheila, but it was also a tough time for her parents. Artie called Joyce, and the two of them met halfway between Carsonville and Lyons to talk face-to-face. It was one of the few times ever told of Artie crying.

She was so upset that Sheila was pregnant. Sheila was also having a relationship with Leon Hummel, whom she did marry, and the beautiful daughter born to her, Kari, took Leon's name. They later had a son, Lance, but divorced soon afterward.

Because Sheila was second born and a girl in a large family, she was responsible for so very much. Aunt Artie was not able to give too much attention to any one person as she had five kids, and then with the others she cared for, one of whom was me, **we all needed to learn to give and help more than we would receive.** Sheila was kind of second in command. Uncle Dutch was busy with his carpentry work and not home much. He also suffered from diabetes, and when he was home, he napped, watched TV, or went to the local restaurant to socialize.

As is the case in many families, my maternal grandmother Eunice, affectionately known as "The General," established and reinforced the matriarchy notion. Aunt Artie wasn't too bossy, but it was passed on to Sheila, as I remember her being quite bossy. So, she just naturally took over and got things done.

Sheila married again, unsuccessfully. She tried to get approval from her parents by meeting expectations that she thought they had for her. She was very dedicated to her many jobs and whatever she threw herself into. One of her characteristics that always came through is the "be there for you" attitude and fortitude. When someone needed help physically or mentally, she was there and continues to be there today. That is one trait that Sheila, Marti, and I got from Aunt Artie.

CHAPTER 6

Beating the Odds or Striking Out

JUST ONE YEAR after Kenny died, March 1961, Dutch experienced a lot of pain, and he drank to self-medicate. His habit quickly developed into alcoholism. The doctors couldn't identify the source of his pain until they sent him to the Veteran's Hospital in Ann Arbor. He had calcium deposits between the inner and outer walls of the pancreas, so it wasn't functioning properly. As far as anyone knew, only five people had ever had a portion of their pancreas removed. Three had lived, two had died, so they gave him about a 50 percent chance of survival. They took out most of his pancreas, leaving him reliant on insulin and creatine from that time on. He was in the hospital for six weeks following the procedure. Dutch was unconscious postoperatively for quite a while. His sisters Katherine and Thelma came to help with the kids while he was recovering.

Nona often took the three-hour round-trip with Ardath to visit Dutch in Ann Arbor. A few times, Joyce came down from her home in Northern Michigan to take Ardath as well. Dutch recovered but still would need lifelong treatment and medication. His doctor told him that he needed to give up alcohol completely, and he did.

His eating became regimented due to the need for regulated insulin levels. Artie always had lunch on the table at noon, and then dinner was ready at 5:00 p.m. Dutch's recovery was long and hard, and his life was changed forever. Just daily life exhausted him, and he would always take naps followed by an early bedtime around 9:00 p.m. The drinking had stopped, but he would often still take the kids to the local bar just to hang out with some of the guys. It was fun for the kids because they always got a Coke and some candy.

In time, the family found some normalcy. In May of 1962, Dutch and Ardath were invited to go to a Tiger's game. It wasn't often they were given a chance to get away, especially without any of the kids. Trying to orchestrate babysitting for five kids is hard enough, but trying to do it for five with three of them having special needs is even more challenging. Luckily, Sheila had just turned 16 and agreed to watch the other kids while her parents went to the baseball game with dear friends Ross and Ester Confer.

Sheila thought it would be a great treat if she loaded all the kids in the car and took them to Ionia for an ice cream cone at the Dairy Queen. Dutch said, "Yes," but Ardath sternly said, "No." Sheila was too new with her license to be hauling all the kids with her anywhere. Sheila was so angry at her mother that she disappeared into the house, hoping to ruin their evening so they couldn't go. Sheila was still small enough that she could slip under her bed. Artie found her, and she ultimately did babysit the kids while her parents left with Ross and Ester.

Sheila was prepared for a late night of being up with the kids. As nighttime fell, she went to sleep in Artie's bed to be close to Scott and Randa. She woke up around 5:00 a.m., and her parents still weren't home, so she knew something was wrong.

Aunt Sandy called her around 7:00 a.m. and told Sheila, "Your mom and dad have been in a terrible accident." Dutch was taken to Lansing General Hospital while Artie was taken by ambulance to Sparrow Hospital, where she remained for six weeks in a full-body cast. Two vehicles collided, and seven people were injured in the accident, so the injured were disbursed to the four hospitals in Lansing. Bob Kilduff, a friend of the family, was the first to come upon the accident. He was the one that got help for them. The accident was near the Williamston exit on I-96. The driver, Ross, was getting tired, and they decided to switch drivers. They stopped on the side of the road when they were hit. The impact of the collision rolled their car, and it landed on its roof in a ditch, where they remained until they were taken to the hospitals.

The family had a hard time finding Ardath. They feared she migh be dead. They even checked the morgue before discovering she was taken to a different hospital.

The next day, Nona drove Sheila to the hospital to see Aunt Artie. She was utterly swollen. Glass was still in her hair, and it was still matted with blood. Nona and Sheila started crying the minute they saw Artie, partly because they were so glad she survived such a hor-rific car accident and partly because she looked so rough.

While Dutch was in the hospital, his sisters, Katherine, Thelma, and Louise, came to stay at the house for the first two weeks. Sheila and Randa stayed with Sandra and Mart and Scott and Mona stayed with Nona and Raymond.

About two weeks after the accident, Dutch was released from the hospital, and he wanted the kids with him. Luckily, it was summer, so he thought that Sheila and Mona could help with Scott and Randa. He seemed to be very ornery over some of the simple things now. He grounded Mona for not hanging up a bathroom towel correctly. Mona and Sheila were always cleaning as Dutch wanted to keep the house up. There were a lot of people stopping in to see the family. And often, they would visit Artie in the hospital.

Artie came home in a body cast that went from the waist down to the knee on her good leg, and the cast went all the way to her toe on her bad leg. She was in a cast for over a year. She tried to run a house-hold, despite the challenges her limited mobility caused. She was still in a cast by the time the kids went back to school. They hired a neigh-bor to come in and help around the house. She came every day when Dutch went off to work to help with the kids and Ardath. There was an agreement that Sally Lyvere, Artie's friend since childhood, and her son, would move in and help. The agreement was supposed to be for a month, but they left suddenly without the family knowing why.

Lollie Mason was a neighbor, and she came every day to check on the family. She offered to help with groceries, laundry, running errands, and more. Artie was on crutches and in a cast forever, it seemed. She went to the doctor and was told that she needed the cast on for another six weeks, and she left, bawling. As luck would have it, she fell down the steps right after she got her cast off and ended up refracturing that leg and had to have another cast.

CHAPTER **7**

A Lesson in Living (& Dying)

AUNT ARTIE WAS my mom's eldest sister. She and her family lived in the same town as Eunice (Grandma) and two of her other sisters. Four of the five girls and their mother lived within a seven-mile radius of one another. For me, that brought a real sense of belonging and security in the tiny town where I grew up. It was a town where everybody knew one another, and you didn't dare raise too much hell because someone, either a relative or a neighbor, was sure to let your folks know what you were up to.

People at the table

The one place where my cousins and friends could go without our folks ever worrying was to Aunt Artie's house. Everybody knew which house belonged to Ardath and Dutch Knepp. It was the big blue house with a huge cement ramp rather than steps out front. Two of Aunt Ardath and Uncle Dutch's kids, my cousins, had muscular dystrophy (MD). Most knew too that they also had a son who died a few years earlier from MD complications.

Everybody knew Uncle Dutch because he had at one time been a meat cutter for our local IGA grocery store and later worked as a carpenter for many local families. One thing they might not have known about Uncle Dutch was that he had a slew of health issues, including diabetes, requiring insulin twice a day.

I know our parents had mixed feelings about us kids always hanging out there. They knew we were safe and happy, but there were also feelings of jealousy that even during our rebellious teen years, it was the place where we all wanted to hang when we didn't want to be at our own homes.

It wasn't that anything immoral or illegal was going on, and it wasn't that her house lacked rules. So, what was it that was drawing so many of the kids there? It was all of the things that made us who we are today. We learned to be accepting of others without judgment. How do you know what someone is going through unless you have walked in their shoes? Physical defects are often easier to identify than mental challenges, but we learned to accept all of them.

Tolerance and patience, these were the most powerful lessons of all. As I live my life today and see how intolerant and impatient people are with one another, it takes me back to the memories in that house. The daily schedules that we each had revolved around Scott and Randa. I look at Randa today and how she has to wait for people to give her each bite of food as she can no longer feed herself. It's remarkable to see the patience she possesses when most of us take seemingly little things like that, or even going to the bathroom alone, for granted. All of these people with MD, kids, young adults, and Randa, now in her 60s, have to wait for people to put them on the bedpan their entire lives to go to the bathroom. Now sustenance, fluid or food, every single drink or bite, needs to be given by another person's hand. For Aunt Artie, helping with Kenny, Scott, and Randa's needs happened every day. She possessed great tolerance and patience, as her children were on the receiving end of her care.

CHAPTER **8**

Rock My World in 18 Months

Grandma Willett

THE MOST IMPACTFUL 18 months of my life rocked my world between 1976 to 1978. In February 1976, my maternal grandmother, Grandma Willett, went to the hospital with a failing heart. She had heart problems for a very long time, and the girls gathered together at the hospital to be with her while she struggled for her life. She passed away on February 9, 1976.

My grandma was a very strong woman. She lost her husband at a very young age and raised those five girls all on her own. **Grandma was the "glue" that held the family together.**

Aunt Artie's HOUSE

Their home is a home
to one and all,
And love surrounds
every wall,
People and animals are
every where,
You can do most things
you dare.
Rules of course there
are to know,
But if you break them
you dont have to go,
Laghts mostly fills the
rooms
At times there is sadness
but hapiness always resumes
It's truly a grand place to be,
I guess it's because love is
the key   - By marti grandchild

Marti's poem

This wasn't something we'd become aware of until well after she was gone.

Nona and Joyce helped Grandma financially in her later years and were the ones to make sure that her financial affairs were settled after she was gone. Grandma never had much to begin with or through-out her life. What was left, the majority went to Ardath, Sandy, and Audrey. Nona and Joyce refused to fight over any of it. I ended up with her coin purse and an Avon candleholder.

I had lots of memories of Grandma as she lived with us for a long time. I always went to Sheila's place to garden with Grandma and helped pick the produce that was ready for "pickin'."

Grandma Willett's death, although not shocking, was still hard as we saw all of the girls struggle through their own grief. There was a lot of anger and sadness, and both seemed to manifest as crying. I know we had lost other family members, but I really hadn't lost anyone I was close to. This was the first one that I have any recollection of. And for all intents and purposes, she was our cornerstone. She was our pillar. They didn't call her "The General" for nothing! She had gained that title because she always knew what to do, and she always barked out orders. And, of course, we all followed those orders. The girls were floundering a bit and trying to get things figured out after she passed.

Aunt Artie knew in her heart that Grandma was not coming home. She sat down with a pen in hand, and in one of her rare quiet mo-ments late one night, she penned a letter to her mother that she knew would never be read. Aunt Artie talked about getting her strength from her mother.

Thursday Morning
February 5, 1976

To a Very Special Mother

My dearest Mom,
You may never get to read
these words Mom, that I'm
going to write.
To me you have been the
best and most wonderful mother
a girl could have. As a young
girl my father was my idol
as he gave in to me and which
you were more strict. As
the years went by I understood.
I'm like that in my father as
I was with my children. But Mom
you were there when I needed
you and you have been the
strength of my life. You showed
me how Mom and I'm

trying to pass it on to my
children and grandchildren.

Dear Mother how I love
you and what fun and good
times we have had. We have
had our problems over the
years but nothing that love
wouldn't overcome. I know
I have never thanked you
enough for what you have done
for me. My thoughts are so
many but words are few. I
think you understand this because
in this way I'm your daughter
two.

Tonight so many memories
come back since I was at least
three years old. Maybe being the
oldest is the rough part but I'm
not sorry as I had you
just a little longer.

I love my sisters dearly. They

each have a special place in my heart and I will continue to try and keep eca together.

Mom, we have weathered many storms of life and I will try to continue to. I can't take your place but I will love your daughters and my sisters as much as possible. You have gave me so much strength through life and if that's all I can give, I think we have accomplished alot in our life time.

You have keep me money wise and that was appreciated but you gave more than that to me. You have taught me to be brave and strong. If I can be just a part of you, I thank God he gave you for my mother.

You have fought all your

life Mom for us girls and our children. I have had bridges to cross some as you and some yet to come. I will do it Mom. You will be beside me. So many thanks Mom for everything. There are no words that can say it all.

At least there is one thing I can say "We picked the last huckleberries together. May you find peace with God and someday I will meet you.

Kenny and Daddy are waiting for you.

With all my love to you, my wonderful mother.

Aunt Artie wrote another letter soon after Grandma died. Both of these letters and the way that Aunt Artie lived her life reflect how deep of a love and appreciation she had for God. It was just the way she lived her life, not a show or for purposes of others to see her go to church. It was who she was and how she lived her own life and what she passed on to all of us.

Mother

Dear God, how much you must have loved me to send me to this particular Mother. This good and beautiful woman who was the source of me. Because she lived, I live, and others live through me. But now you have taken her back to yourself, and I am bereft. The ~~hurt~~ hurt is intolerable; I want her as I did as a child when something went wrong. I feel as I must run through the world, calling, "Mother, Mother, where are"? As I ran crying through the house, sometimes as a little girl. "Here dear, I'm right here." She would say, appearing Or, returning from an errand, "My goodness honey, I've been gone for a short time." And now, even as I call out to her, I feel her presence. It's as if she put her arms around me as she used to,

or is streaking my hair and
comforting, " Don't cry, honey,
its alright, I'm right here. You
know I would never leave you
alone for very long."

Dear Gram,

I love you so much and miss you dearly. Right at this moment I just wonder what kind of children you brought into this world. Maybe that's what they still are; children. Since you've gone they have become so immature and self-centered. I know how you held the family together so well and I wish it could still be the same way again. Somehow, the love we knew has turned into arguments and bitterness. It's not fair that we should have it taken away in a year's time because of Death. I had never realized how much Death could affect people. Our family has let Death overcome them. The strength you gave to us is being used not to keep love and a happy family life, but a

Constant fight between your girls. Please don't ever let your grandchildren ever become so imbittered about this past year, years before, and years to come. Let God give us the understanding and patience with each other like we knew once before. Gram, I love you and thanks for letting me write to you and for listening.

Marti

Uncle Dutch

My uncle Dutch died suddenly from an aneurysm on March 27, 1976. He was gone so quickly there wasn't much time to do any grieving and certainly no time to say goodbye. The days rolled into one another, and there were so many things to be done. I was much too young to really understand it all. I was only 12 years old, and none of the family went to church or even talked about God. I just knew that there had to be something good out of this. My aunt Artie slumped over on the couch with her head in her hands, trying to be strong. The temperature outside was so cold, and the house seemed even colder on that day. They never had carpeting in the house because of the wheelchairs, so the tile didn't help with how cold it got during the winter months. One day, I was just staring at the grout in the tile, trying to remember how he called my name or the naps he took daily. We always had to be quiet during that time of day. How can I hold onto all those memories? Will we ever be okay?

The winter months passed like we were all walking on eggshells. **Every day seemed to be more painful than the last one, and we had more of a burden than we did the day before.** Especially Aunt Artie. Not that Uncle Dutch helped that much with the kids, but he brought home the money for bills and provided her with companionship. The two never slept together because Aunt Artie always slept in a double bed downstairs with Scott right beside her and Randa in a hospital bed with a bedside table in between, but she always knew he was there. Right upstairs. He would climb the stairs and retire to his bedroom every evening. She would hear the creak of the floors or the running of the water as he prepared for bed. All those things had been a comfort that was different from what most of us think of, but for Aunt Artie, those things were the simple validations that she wasn't alone even into the wee hours of the morning.

After Uncle Dutch died, the nights and days just became longer. Her nights of being awakened by the kids increased. I think they all were restless most of the time. Scott would wake her up and ask her to roll him over or stretch him out a little. Their dear hearts and their ravaged bodies seemed to be taxed so much more as the months went on.

CHAPTER **9**

Don't Lie to Me

LESS THAN 10 months after Uncle Dutch died, Scott came down with pneumonia and ended up in the hospital. I was old enough to know that everyone was extremely worried, so I asked Marti and Randa about Scott when they called me from the hospital. "Is he coming home? Is he going to be all right?" I asked frantically. "Yes, he is fine and will be coming home soon," they told me. I just needed some reassurance to be put at ease. Since Uncle Dutch died, our lives had been in such discord that I just wanted Scott to come home and be all right.

Well, Scott didn't come home. He died in the hospital. My mom crawled into bed with him and told him not to be scared and that everything would be fine; just relax. They had put him in an oxygen tent to give him a breathing treatment. In the background, the doctors had been talking with Aunt Artie about doing a tracheotomy. How could they do a tracheotomy on him? His voice and imagination were all he had. He couldn't walk, he couldn't do much, and now they were thinking about taking away his voice. My mother crawled out of Scott's bed and stepped out into the hallway to talk to Aunt Artie about going to the chapel so she could pray. Aunt Artie was falling apart. My mom couldn't hold her up and keep Scott calm at the same time.

Aunt Artie went to the chapel to have some private time. I am not sure if she asked for help, answers, or strength, but whatever it was, she came back with a sense of calmness. She was able to make the decision not to let them do a tracheotomy on Scott.

Scott died from complications of pneumonia on January 4, 1977.

They lied to me. They told me he would be okay. They came back to the house and told me Scott had died. All I remember as an almost 13-year-old was heading upstairs and stopping halfway up the landing, unable to catch my breath. I was crying so hard that I was hyperventilating. I was so angry . . . angry . . . *angry*! I was angry at God; I was angry at Marti and Randa for lying to me. How could there be a God? How could he take our Scott?

I remember going back to my parents' house for the next few nights and crying myself to sleep. It was so hard to understand and comprehend this loss. I really don't remember the funeral. Scott's passing was especially hard for Randa. He was the only person that truly knew how she felt, that fought the same fight she fought every single day of her life—the fight to stay alive! She was now alone. Aunt Artie lost yet another child only 10 months after losing her husband and a year after her mother's passing.

Randa talked about the deep, dark path that Aunt Artie lived for quite a few years after all the death. Within the same 18 months, some of the loyal pets that were also companions to her and us kids succumbed to death, adding to this gaping void in our lives. Randa told us how Aunt Artie would go through the motions of the day but did not do a lot of talking and showed very little affection. She would lie down for a nap every day just to pass the time, longing for some of the dreams or a glimpse of her loved ones no longer physically with her. Randa said it was if she felt she were more of a burden than before as Aunt Artie didn't want to live. Randa just kept pushing her. She tried everything to help with filling the crater left in their hearts and lives. Randa brought in stray animals, although they seemed also to have special needs and required more work. To Aunt Artie, again, it didn't matter. She loved them, and it made her smile once more.

I had my own demons. I no longer believed in God. How could God do this to her—to us—to *me*! At 13, it was all about me. My whole world had been rocked. Part of the sadness of those deaths was the loss of people that "I was special" to. My aunt Artie was still alive, but her walls were up. I could feel it.

Life did move on, and we tried to keep some of the same traditions going. Grandma had always been the catalyst during Thanksgiving, but that changed. **We really never got back together as an entire family again for a Thanksgiving after she died.** Nona tried to fill the shoes of "The General," but most of the family resented that and thought it was a little too soon for her to be taking control. The girls struggled with their relationships with one another, and their whole dynamic seemed to have shifted.

Audrey and Rodney had the most consistency. They moved through it and kept themselves and the two boys in their close-knit family moving through life. Aunt Sandy and Uncle Mart struggled with their relationship more. I think that Aunt Sandy felt the loss so much more as she really never knew her dad, given that she was so young when he died, and now, losing her mother made her dependence on

Uncle Mart all that more necessary in her mind. She had also started relying on prescription drugs for coping with life in general.

Joyce and Russ seemed to have a little more independence. Joyce always tried to make trips down from Northern Michigan to help Grandma keep the family together, but this was almost a permission she had been seeking to live a little more freely with Uncle Russ. They started traveling more.

Nona and Raymond were pretty consistent with their involvement with the Knepps and with the other family members. As described before, Nona thought it was her place to bring the family together and be in charge. I remember her many times at the table mourning for the loss of her mother. I know she felt a very, very significant loss when she died.

Aunt Artie had been the one with the most loss, burying all three of them in 18 months.

CHAPTER **10**

Don't Leave Me; I'm Not Ready

OUR LIVES MOVED forward. Us "kids" grew up out of our teens and into young adulthood. Aunt Artie and Randa became more self-reliant together. Although whenever possible, Aunt Joyce, Uncle Russ, Mom and Dad, Aunt Audrey, Uncle Rodney, and Aunt Sandy and Uncle Mart would help financially when they could and found ways to support them in other ways as they were able. The kids, Marti, Sheila, Mona, and I, along with our husbands, were the ones that helped the most. We may not have supported them much financially, but we always tried to help fill the void.

As we began to have our own children, that too was a huge help. **Artie had so much love to give.** We would show up on the weekends and play cards, have a few snacks, some pop, and lots of laughs. It seemed like forever, but there was a point in time that spanned over a few years where Aunt Artie didn't enjoy music because every song held memories for her. It was really strange because we had always listened to music. Randa accumulated hundreds of albums, and we would sit for hours upon hours listening to them and learning all the lyrics. After the painfully long period of a music-less house, it was good to hear the music and sing with each other once again. Aunt Artie's favorite was always Neil Diamond. She would be in the kitchen doing dishes or making supper, and her body would be moving to the music. Sometimes she would shake and move into the living room for a little dance session, music blaring loud enough that all the neighbors could hear, but we didn't care.

The Jerry Lewis Telethons had always been something that we looked forward to and planned on from year to year. We held fundraisers over a handful of the years, but we always, *always* got together at the Knepps. Every year, we kept track of people that called or stopped by. It was so good to see our friends, family, and community come together every single year to support the fight against MD. It was a 24-hour telethon that was explicitly for muscular dystrophy. At the end of the telethon, the song that Jerry Lewis would always sing was "You Will Never Walk Alone." It was always a killer way to end the event. **There would never be a dry eye in the house.**

Aunt Artie had a chandelier in her living room above the TV. Year after year, we always hung our bras there when it was time to settle in for the evening. We could identify all who were staying there! It was funny because every year as the girls grew up, the number of bras increased.

The things to look forward to had always been limited due to having kids with basic infantile needs. As the years passed with everything being on Randa and Aunt Artie, it must have felt to Artie that she finally caught a small break. It was easier to just take care of one . . . Randa. We had grown up learning how to put them on the bedpans and then "swing" them back into their chairs. Of course, feeding them was easy, and often, as we got older, we could put Randa in the van and go places. That freedom was there for Aunt Artie too. She would play cards or Bingo at the Moose Lodge and do a little gambling once in a while. I don't know if she was ever away for more than four or five days, but at least she was getting out a little bit more.

One day in September of 1992, I received a phone call. Aunt Artie had a stroke. I went to meet Sheila and Randa at Ingham Hospital in Lansing. The trip was fairly easy for me as I had moved to Okemos with the girls. It was just a matter of finding a sitter on such short notice. All I knew was that I *needed* to go. I made friends with the young couple next door to me at our apartment, so I went over and knocked on the door with tears in my eyes. They gladly said they would watch the girls and assured me I could take as long as I needed at the hospital, and they would take care of everything at home.

My mind was swirling with thoughts, feelings, memories, and dread. How bad was it? Was she going to be all right? When I got to the hospital, everyone was talking. They talked over each other and wanted to tell the story of the day and what had happened. I wanted to hear, really I did, yet I couldn't. I just wanted to see her. I *needed* to see her.

A few hours went by before they finally got her stabilized, and we kissed each other goodbye for the night. They all left and went home. I still needed to be with my aunt Artie. I asked if I could go into her room, and the nurse said I could. I remember it as if it were yesterday. She was tired. She looked old for the first time. It was a major stroke, and it left her unresponsive. I remember rehearsing in my head what I was going to say to her. I didn't want to lose her. I wasn't ready. I still needed her! She held strength for so many people year after year, and I told her that I understood if she was tired. If she needed to go, that she could, but I wasn't ready. I figured she could probably hear me, so I tried my hardest to be strong and not let my fear or sadness come through in my voice. I needed her to stay calm, and this was something that she needed to want to fight for. This was between her and God. I could only pray and be there for support if and when she regained consciousness. **It was a comfort to believe in God again.**

I stayed well into the early-morning hours. I couldn't bear to leave Aunt Artie alone. I sat quietly and prayed for her and, quite frankly, prayed for myself and our family.

I went home to be with the girls and slept for a few hours. Then I sent them off for school, and I got myself ready for work. I made it through the workday, but at lunchtime, I checked on Aunt Artie. I went again after work after I picked up the girls. She finally regained consciousness, but we knew it would be a long haul to regain functionality. Her entire left side was affected by the stroke. This went on for several weeks, so my routine changed. I woke up early in the morning, took the girls to before-school daycare, went to the hospital to help her eat, get dressed, and go to the bathroom. The mornings always felt rushed before heading to work. At lunchtime each day, I went back to the hospital to help her brush her hair, teeth, and do a few exercises to facilitate rehabilitation. Evenings, I picked up the girls before I'd go back to the hospital to see her, all the while rooting for her to get better and wanting to survive. The regimen was exhausting, but it felt good being able to support her in those ways.

Two weeks after Aunt Artie's stroke, Uncle Mart had a heart attack and was in the hospital across town at Sparrow. Aunt Artie had the wherewithal to know that she wanted to be there for her sister, Sandy, the baby of the family. Uncle Mart was going to have dialysis, and that was a hard pill for him to swallow. I think he just gave up. He died on October 12, 1992, and was buried on October 15th. Aunt Artie was still in the hospital and missed the funeral.

Aunt Artie never said much either way. It was a long way back for her to any real level of functioning. Her left side was left in a permanent state of paralysis. A few years went by, and she came to stay with my husband and our family. She kept apologizing because I had to help her with so much, even going to the bathroom.

She taught us that this is the circle of life.

She took such good care of us, taught us so well, and now, it was my turn to help her. I made her smile, but it was hard for her. Often, when she and I were together, we called Aunt Joyce so that she had a chance to talk with her. Aunt Artie would lay the phone down and drift off to whatever was going on around her. She was never the same. She was there in body, but never really the Aunt Artie that we knew. We all took care of her and accepted her, but it must have been so hard. There she was, needing a caregiver to help with *her* needs and care after Randa as well. Now, what she had been doing all her adult life in taking care of her children . . . was now what she needed most.

Aunt Artie passes on.

On the night of February 4, 2001, Aunt Artie joined her husband in death. A few days earlier, she had spoken wistfully about wanting to dance with him again. Randa, Mona, and Sheila were by her side all that day. She went in and out of consciousness throughout the day and into the night. Around 11:30 p.m., Randa whispered to her that it was "okay to go and be with Daddy." Randa and Mona went to the kitchen to get a cup of coffee to strengthen Randa during the vigil. When Sheila and Mona returned to Aunt Artie's side at 11:45 p.m., she was gone. Aunt Artie passed from this world to the next in the loving care of her daughters, Randa, Mona, and Sheila.

Sheila, Artie and Randa

Nona and Artie

On the beach

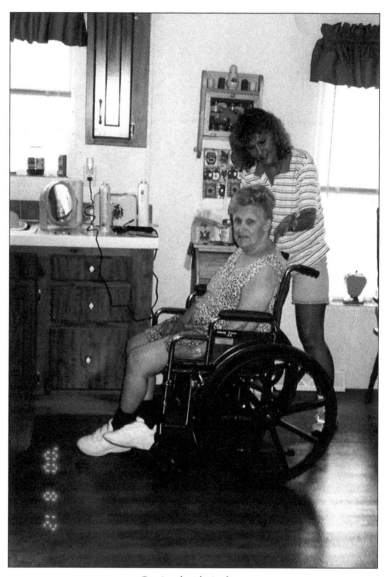

Getting her hair done

CHAPTER 11

Sifting Through the Memories and the Stuff

COFFEE. THE SMELL of coffee was coming from the kitchen. Colleen got up as soon as she heard the dogs barking and started a pot of coffee for us. When we emerged from Randa's bedroom, Colleen gave us both a welcoming hug before she and Marti immediately lit up a cigarette.

I headed to the cupboard for cups to go around, then the refrigerator for creamer. Marti and I had held off on stopping to get something to eat because we were anxious to get there. I knew that soon after coffee, we would have to get a bite to eat before we met up with Mona.

My nervousness is usually handled by making my hands busy, as we were taught. Busy hands, happy heart! I immediately started making a grocery list as the two of them sat there, dragging on their cigarettes. It was hard to wrap my mind around the fact that my aunt had died of lung cancer, and here, almost the entire family still smoked. All but Sheila and I were smokers in our family circle.

After they were through with their cigarettes, Colleen headed in to put Randa on the "pot," and Marti and I headed to the grocery store. About an hour and a half later, we returned with our arms loaded with bags of food. We were greeted with gratitude and excitement as we pulled out "treats" of candy, soda pop, chips, meat, and much more. It was a little overwhelming, but we knew that they had been struggling to make ends meet, and we wanted to take care of them while we were there. Breakfast turned more into a junk food feast. We decided that we needed to do whatever it took to get through it.

It was probably about 10:00 a.m. before we called Mona's house. She lived about three miles up the road from Aunt Artie and Randa, so it wasn't too far. Aunt Artie and Randa had put a lot of stuff into Mona and Ken's pole barn when they moved to Oklahoma. That was some of the things we needed to go through, as well as the stuff at the house.

When Mona got there, we rehashed many things. **Memories were the hardest thing about her death.** We all felt so guilty because, you see, Aunt Artie wanted to be buried in the cemetery beside her loved ones: her sons, Scott and Kenny, as well as her husband, Dutch. However, when Aunt Artie was on her deathbed, and discussions took place about what to do after she was gone, it all came out just how bleak the situation was. There really wasn't any money. Aunt Artie didn't have a life insurance policy, and there wasn't a stash of cash in the freezer or under the mattress or in the cookie jar. All that was in the cookie jar were cookies! How were we going to get her body back to Michigan, where she wanted to be? Well, the not-so-obvious answer was that she would have to be cremated. That was a hard pill to swallow as it was not what she wanted, but it seemed that it was the only logical way of getting her back to Michigan. I tried to plan it like "Little Miss Sunshine" with Grandpa and putting Aunt Artie in the back of my suburban and dragging her dead body across state lines, but the rest of my family and my husband were not on board with that one.

It was truly one of the times that I just wanted to be rebellious—just do it and ask for forgiveness later. But too many people would know about it, so I couldn't just sneak her out. Everything would have been okay, but we were all so burdened with guilt. Do we tell her while she is on her deathbed, or do we wait until after she is gone and just do it? Well, Randa decided that Artie needed to know what we were going to do, so she told her. That morning, we rehashed some of those decisions and what do with her *now*. You see, now, *she* was in the cookie jar! Yep, Aunt Artie was in the Red Strawberry Cookie Jar. That was her urn; that is what we chose. Well, the cookie jar wouldn't be too hard to get back to Michigan, but we needed to plan some type of a service that we could have to honor Ardath Ruth Fenn Knepp.

It is so hard to believe that she had left such a legacy and every-thing that we are, everything that we possess, gets down to, as our priest distributes the ashes in Lent: "Remember, you are dust, and unto dust you shall return." And so the day went on. We pulled out her jew-elry box and divided up her jewelry and talked about every piece. Her material possessions were few, and what she did have, the value was only sentimental. Most of everything she had was very old and often was handed down to her from Grandma Willett or Great-grandma.

I had made her several items that she treasured and held onto until the day she died. I made a key holder for her out of a "ball and paddle." The paddle was actually the key holder that I decorated and shellacked. I made her a ceramic cherub that she had in her bedroom that reminded me of her. As the years passed and I was able to buy her a few things, one of those was a music box that displayed "Footprints in the Sand":

Marti, Colleen, Randa

That poem reminded me of Aunt Artie and how she must have felt so many times in her life. She "carried" all of us when we felt alone, and God carried her. **She did not often speak of God, but she lived the life!**

We made Sloppy Joe sandwiches and sat down to eat lunch with a plan to go to Mona's, where we sorted through the things in the pole barn. Ken had opened the big door to give us as much light as possible. Fortunately, it was a beautiful day. The sun was shining, and the air was crisp with the smell of fall. The sky was filled with wispy, white clouds.

As we walked into the barn, the smell of hay and dust stung my nose. Right away, I noticed Scott's old table. Wow, it had been so many years since I had seen that table. It was a drop-leaf table that my mom had refinished for him. Scott used to lie on the table with a foam pad on it. He spent many, many hours on that table, and now, it was just dusty old furniture that had been discarded. It had a lot of meaning. My mom had refinished it, but more importantly—Scott! Scott spent a large amount of his last few years on that table with me sitting beside him in a chair, playing with his Wild, Wild West characters, playing board games, or pretending to be a Star Trek character. We loaded the table in the truck to take it back to Michigan to see if it could be repaired.

We got the Christmas decorations but decided that Mona and Randa would keep most of those in Oklahoma. Holding onto memories of the past was always important to Marti. We both treasure things because of the sentiment more than anything else, but Marti is a little overboard about it. When you walk into her house, it's like stepping back in time. She has collected items from all sides of her history, and everything is a treasure to her. She has baby dolls, art, bottles filled with colored water, artificial flowers, family pictures, hand-me-down furniture, tools, and more.

When Marti's parents passed away at a relatively early age, she was the recipient of most of their items. Well, when Marti saw an old card table that was warped in the middle, it flooded so many memories for all of us, but especially for Marti. She spent many hours playing with Barbie dolls on the front porch of Aunt Artie's house on that card table. **She *had* to have that card table!** I made fun of her, as I usually did! I asked her what she was going to do with it. It wasn't like we didn't have plenty of room in the Suburban to take it home, but where was she going to put it when she got home, and what in the world was she going to use it for? Whatever, it meant a lot to her, so it got loaded in the Suburban.

There was the old rocking chair that Grandma Willett had bought, one for Aunt Artie and one for Aunt Joyce. Aunt Artie's was here in the barn. It needed a lot of TLC, but it was one of the things that Aunt

Artie had taken the time to write down that was supposed to go to me, so that got loaded up too.

Aunt Artie had her favorite color sprinkled throughout the house. Red dishes, red refrigerator, pots and pans, hand towels, and so much more that had been packed in boxes were also there in storage. That stuff was divided up between Sheila and Marti. Both of them were thrilled to be the recipients of those items that were treasured and used every single day of her life, as well as ours. **The cookie jar we had already found a home for!** Material things never really meant a lot to Aunt Artie. Why would they?

CHAPTER 12

Where We Are Today—
The Legacy Lives On

WHEN I WAS born on that sunny day on July 10, 1964, most of the influences that would shape the person I am, and still strive to be, were already in place. My mother's family, including my grandma, my aunt Sandy and her family, and my aunt Artie and her family, lived several blocks from me.

At only six weeks old, my life with my second mother became a part of my daily routine. It was with my aunt Artie I learned to walk, talk, and I truly blossomed. Little would I realize she would teach the lessons about living and dying that I would take with me throughout my own life experiences and challenges.

I was blessed with an extended family that surrounded me. My dad's mother lived several blocks west of the house I grew up in until age 16. My dad's only sister lived about four blocks south with her two kids as well.

My mom's mother lived next door to my dad's sister and my aunt Sandy. My mom's baby sister lived with her husband and two kids only two blocks from my grandma Sprague. **My greatest gift was my mom's eldest sister, Aunt Artie, who became my second mother.** She lived with my uncle Dutch, cousins Sheila, Mona, Randa, and Scott, in a house only three blocks from my parents.

There was a real sense of belonging and security in the tiny town where I grew up. It was a town where everybody knew one another, and you didn't dare raise too much heck because someone, either a relative or a neighbor, was sure to let your folks know what you were up to.

The one place where my cousins and friends could go without our folks every worrying was Aunt Artie's house. Everybody knew which house belonged to Ardath and Dutch Knepp. It was the big blue house with a huge cement ramp rather than steps in front. Ardath and Dutch had five kids, my cousins, three of whom had muscular dystrophy. Most everyone knew they also had a son who had died a few years before from MD complications.

Everybody had met Uncle Dutch at one time or another as he had been a meat cutter for our local IGA store and later worked as a carpenter for many local families. One thing they might not have known about Uncle Dutch was he had a slew of health issues, including diabetes, requiring insulin twice daily.

I know our parents had mixed feelings about our hanging out there. They knew we were safe and happy, but there were also feelings of jealousy that, even during our rebellious teen years, it was the place where we all wanted to be.

It wasn't that anything immoral or illegal had gone on, and it wasn't that her house lacked rules. So, what was it that drew so many of the kids there? Fleetwood Mac's "Go Your Own Way" was playing on the stereo. We would listen to the entire *Rumours* album. That would be followed by Boz Scaggs's *Silk Degrees*. Suddenly, Aunt Artie would yell to Randa and me to play some Rod Stewart or Dire Straits.

Our folks knew we often played cards or games and listened to music. We drank sun tea or coffee. **We discussed our latest summer love or our winter heartbreaks.** They also knew we could be doing any combination of these things at any of our homes. In fact, most of us had a great deal of freedom in our homes because all our parents worked during the day. Really, there were fewer restrictions at home because there was no adult supervision.

As young teens, I don't know if we even could put our own fingers on exactly why we were so drawn to the house. We only know that it's where we belonged and where we had a sense of contentment. **Merely being there made us happy.** As an adult, I've contemplated the attraction. We didn't realize it consciously at the time, but we were students of life in that house.

I remember devising a cheer for Forest Grove, a special education school. It wasn't about making fun of the mentally or physically challenged but finding the humor in those challenges. We learned there are always limits. As accepting as the atmosphere was, we couldn't use the "F" word. No one could call anyone names. It became commonplace to tell someone they were a "BRT" because you couldn't refer to any kid as a "brat." You could complain about your parents, but you couldn't cross the line into disrespect toward them. And it was not okay to discuss family issues that your parents insisted belonged in your home.

Research today shows the benefits of naps. We always had been taught that. As children, we all took naps. Aunt Artie always did as well, even as an adult. We learned it took a village to raise a child. **The more people who love your kids, the more adjusted and secure everyone felt.**

There is always someone worse off than you. You can't wallow in self-pity. You still must get up every day. Tears and death are part of the natural order of life. As traumatic as death could be, there was laughter to get you through, and sometimes, there were worse things than death. We learned that growing old is a state of mind if you chose to remain stuck in your time period rather than adapt to changes, and that changes weren't bad. They were just a natural consequence of time passing.

It is important to give. You might not be able to afford to give financially, but you can give the gift of yourself . . . your time, your talents, or your listening ear. One of the greatest gifts is to open your heart and home to family and friends. You take people in when they need structure, safety, and a sense of belonging.

We learned that animals were creatures of God, and being cruel to them is never acceptable. We learned the sanctity of family. You can't hate. What you have might not be the best, but you take care of it. Find the small joys, just like when we didn't have power, and we went sliding down the ramp on the ice during an ice storm.

Simple things—Vacations weren't to Europe or on cruises. It was who you were with. The best times were at the cabin without electricity and running water. We had gaslights, and we pumped our water. We didn't have a TV or VCR. All meals were homemade. We picked wild huckleberries and mint. **We were surrounded by love.**

We learned poker and math lessons. We played with pennies, nickels, and dimes. We learned how to keep a poker face. Sometimes you were up, and sometimes you were down.

The ones that are most important today are Randa and Aunt Joyce. Randa is 66 and had done her best to live on and through Aunt Artie.

Scott and Randa

Randa

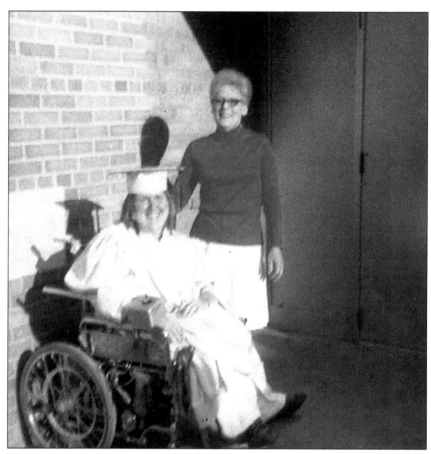

Randa graduating

Randa looking hot

Randa, Marti and Sarah

Randa, Sheila and Sarah, stuck in elevator in Vegas

In Vegas for Randa's 50th

One of Randa's strongest qualities is her stubbornness, and if it weren't for that, she wouldn't be alive today. She has weathered through all of life's challenges with determination, resilience, patience, kindness, compassion, and so many more of Artie's qualities. Randa's outer shell is sometimes hard to break through, as she has had to have it to protect herself. If she were weak and allowed herself to be hurt by everyone and everything, she wouldn't have survived as long as she has.

Not only has she been a thriving, working individual for the state of Michigan, but many, many other jobs as well. When Artie had her stroke, it took quite a toll on Randa. She took a leave of absence, eventually retiring from the state. She became the caretaker for her mother, overseeing the different people coming into their home to care for them. Sheila moved in with them for a while to help. Over the next few years, over three dozen caregivers would come through the family home.

CHAPTER 13

Test of Faith

THERE ARE SO many times in life when we ask ourselves . . . Why? What was the purpose? What was the plan because it certainly wasn't our plan? These questions arose for many of us in the family, and they were asked many times over. It never was Aunt Artie who asked, just the rest of us. Sometime toward the end of 2000, Aunt Artie was diagnosed with cancer. My brother Kevin never really talked about God much or had any spiritual tendencies, but this was one time in my life that I remember Kevin being mad at God. I was 10 years younger than he and much closer to Aunt Artie and in my spiritual relationship with God, as well. So, I counseled Kevin. But it was very difficult for me. We had over eight years more than I expected with Aunt Artie. It wasn't how I would have chosen the last eight years of her life to be, but it was what it was. Now, it was time to make sure that she was comfortable, and for once, it was clear what we could do to help her.

Thank You, Aunt Artie

The lessons we learned from her were about patience, acceptance, and unconditional love. We learned to appreciate the joy that can come from music. We learned to face challenges with dignity and humor. We learned to laugh at ourselves. We discovered that we were all handicapped in some way. But the handicap didn't have to limit you, and it certainly wasn't an excuse. She taught us to carry the belief inside that life was a gift, and that it could be taken away at any time, so you'd better appreciate what you have been given. We learned there was very little that was so sacred that you couldn't laugh about it. Aunt Artie had an unshakeable belief that heartache could be met with laughter.

Appendix I

What Is Muscular Dystrophy?

Muscular dystrophy is a broad term used to label gene-related disorders that affect muscles throughout the body. There are more than 20 specific genetic disorders considered to be muscular dystrophy. Most have the same result (a reduction in muscle strength due to weakening and deterioration), but these various types of muscular dystrophies are specific to different muscles in the body and different rates of degeneration.

Duchenne muscular dystrophy (DMD) is perhaps the most common type of muscular dystrophy in existence. Since it was first identified in the 1860s, DMD affects approximately one in every 3,000 boys. Another type of muscular dystrophy associated with DMD is Becker muscular dystrophy (BMD). Since its first diagnosis in the 1950s, Becker MD occurs in about one in 18,000 births and is considered to be a less severe form of DMD.

What Causes Muscular Dystrophy?

There is a vital muscle protein called "dystrophin within our genetic makeup," which is one of the largest genes found to date. Dystrophin acts as the glue that holds muscles together by maintaining the structure of muscle cells. Dystrophin is also believed to carry signals between the inside and outside of muscle fibers. Without dystrophin, muscles are not able to operate properly and will eventually suffer progressive damage.

The dystrophin gene is carried on the X chromosome. Males are, therefore, more susceptible to dystrophin damage because they have only one X chromosome. When a boy is diagnosed with DMD, his body is not able to produce any dystrophin. In Becker MD, a distorted, oversized version of dystrophin is generated. In either disorder, muscle cells within the body gradually weaken and eventually die without fully functional dystrophin.
Kenny had spinal muscular atrophy.

Spinal muscular atrophy is a group of inherited diseases that cause progressive muscle degeneration and weakness, eventually leading to death.

Causes, incidence, and risk factors:

Spinal muscular atrophy (SMA) is a collection of different muscle diseases. Grouped together, it is the second leading cause of neuromuscular disease. Most of the time, a person must get the defective gene from both parents to be affected. Approximately four out of every 100,000 people have the condition.

The most severe form is SMA Type I, also called Werdnig-Hoffman disease. Infants with SMA Type II have less severe symptoms during early infancy, but they become progressively weaker with time. SMA Type III is the least severe form of the disease.

Rarely, SMA may begin in adulthood. This is usually a milder form of the disease. A family history of spinal muscular atrophy is a risk factor for all types of the disorder.

Symptoms:

Infants with SMA Type I are born with very little muscle tone, weak muscles, and feeding and breathing problems. With SMA Type III, symptoms may not appear until the second year of life. Often, weakness is first noted in the shoulder muscles and proximal leg muscles. Weakness gets worse over time and will become severe.

Symptoms in an infant:

- Breathing difficulty
- Feeding difficulty
- Floppy infant (poor muscle tone)
- Lack of head control
- Little spontaneous movement
- Progressive weakness (older infant to toddler)

Symptoms in a child:

- Frequent, increasingly severe respiratory infections
- Nasal speech
- Worsening posture

CPSIA information can be obtained
at www.ICGtesting.com
Printed in the USA
LVHW011950231221
706909LV00010B/187

9 781977 232298